There
a Scottish Pa

Frances and Gordon Jarvie

SCOTTIES SERIES EDITORS
Frances and Gordon Jarvie

Contents

Published in 2013 by
NMS Enterprises Limited – Publishing
a division of NMS Enterprises Limited
National Museums Scotland
Chambers Street, Edinburgh EH1 1JF

ISBN: 978-1-905267-61-3

British Library Cataloguing in Publication Data
A catalogue record of this book is available from the British Library.

Book design concept by Redpath.
Cover design by Mark Blackadder.
Layout by NMS Enterprises Limited – Publishing.
Printed and bound in the United Kingdom by Bell & Bain Ltd, Glasgow.

CREDITS

The authors wish to thank Ian McCracken of Govan High School, Glasgow, for highlighting relevant details in the national Curriculum for Excellence; and the Records of the Parliaments of Scotland project based at the University of St Andrews.

Thanks are due to the individuals and organisations who supplied images and photographs for this publication. Every attempt has been made to contact copyright holders to use the material in this publication. If any image has been inadvertently missed, please contact the publisher.

COVER ILLUSTRATIONS

Front cover, above: The Scottish Parliament illuminated at night (© 2005 Scottish Parliamentary Corporate Body). Below: detail from The Riding of the Parliament, 1685 (© National Museums Scotland). Back cover: Lighting through the Garden Lobby roof (© 2009 Scottish Parliamentary Corporate Body).

FURTHER CREDITS (p. viii of Facts and activities section).

For a full listing of NMS Enterprises Limited – Publishing titles and related merchandise:
www.nms.ac.uk/books

What was the Parliament of Scotland?

Parliaments existed in Scotland, off and on, from about 1200 until 1707.

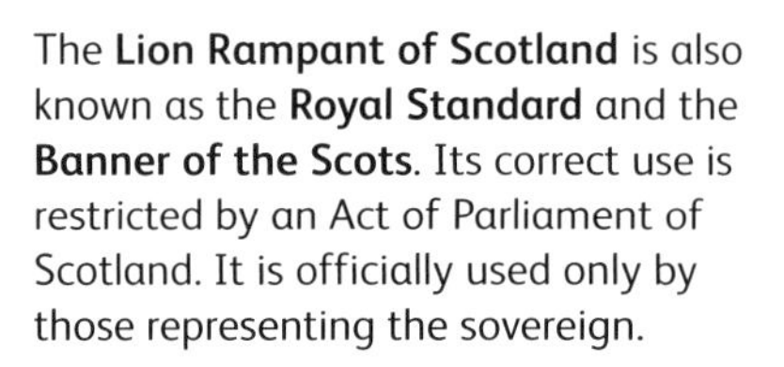

The **Lion Rampant of Scotland** is also known as the **Royal Standard** and the **Banner of the Scots**. Its correct use is restricted by an Act of Parliament of Scotland. It is officially used only by those representing the sovereign.

In their earliest days, records in Latin spoke of a *colloquium*, meaning 'a conversation' or 'a place of conversation', that took place at Kirkliston, near Edinburgh. This was in 1235, during the reign of King Alexander II. Membership of the Parliament was made up of the **Estates**, or communities, of the Realm.

The **First Estate** was made up of important men of the Church, people like bishops or abbots.

The **Second Estate** comprised lairds and noblemen.

By about 1325, in the time of King Robert the Bruce, burgess representatives of the royal burghs were appointed. These people were often commoners. This was the start of the **Third Estate**, and it was to grow in influence and importance over the centuries.

In some countries (England, for example) the Parliament was *bicameral*, or made up of two houses: a House of Commons, for representatives from the boroughs and shires; and a House of Lords, for the bishops (the 'princes of the church') and nobility. However, in Scotland the Parliament was *unicameral*, or made up of one house. All **Three Estates** met together in a single assembly.

From earliest days debates were soon dominated by the king's need to raise money. He needed money to defend himself and his kingdom. He needed to raise an army or navy, to build strong castles, and to reward his supporters (often with bribes!). He needed the Parliament to make laws, and – much harder in those lawless times – he needed money to try to implement these laws throughout his realm.

Just as the king was in the habit of travelling the length and breadth of his kingdom, the Parliament also moved about the realm. In addition to Edinburgh and Kirkliston, Parliaments were also held at Stirling and Linlithgow, Perth, St Andrews, Dundee, Dunfermline, Glasgow, Aberdeen, Inverness, Arbroath and Berwick-upon-Tweed.

The Great Hall, or Parliament Hall, at Stirling Castle was built by King James IV in 1500. It is the finest surviving medieval hall in Scotland. The only 'permanent' home enjoyed by the Parliament of Scotland was the Parliament Hall, on the High Street in Edinburgh, commissioned by King Charles I and completed in 1639.

The Parliament Hall at Stirling Castle, showing the magnificent hammer-beam ceiling. The inset focuses on the royal arms of Scotland.

Other early parliaments

Witan

The Witan, or Witenagemot, was the Anglo-Saxon meeting of wise men who advised England's Anglo-Saxon kings before 1066 – people like King Alfred the Great.

Thing

The Norsemen or Vikings had an assembly called a Thing. Iceland had the earliest Thing (at Thingvellir). Scotland's Vikings had several Things (place-names like Dingwall – or Thingwall – and Tingwall in Shetland tell us this). The Manx Parliament to this day sits at a place called Tynwald, again from the root word 'Thing'.

Ireland's Parliament

The Parliament in Ireland dated from around the same time as the English and Scottish ones. But the English soon insisted that all acts of the Irish Parliament be rubber-stamped by the English Parliament.

'Maist things hae a sma beginning ...'

What does the word 'parliament' mean to you?

Why do we need a parliament?

Make a mind map of any words or terms used in a parliament.

Kings and Guardians of the Realm

In 1306, twenty years after the death of King Alexander III, King Robert I, popularly known as Robert the Bruce, seized the Scottish throne.

A re-enactment, on 6 April 2010, of the signing of the Declaration of Arbroath as part of Angus Council's celebration of Tartan Week, 690 years from the original signing.

His reign got off to a shaky start, and he was hunted up and down the land by the English. But after his victory at Bannockburn in 1314, it became clear that he would use the Scottish Parliament as a sort of royal 'rubber stamp'. Royal authority was thus restored. This reduced the Parliament's role to approving the king's decisions in accordance with Scots law.

The most memorable of these acts was the famous Declaration of Arbroath (1320), where Robert held a Parliament on 6th April. Many people signed this Declaration, because the king understood that the idea of authority vested in 'the community of the realm' was a very strong one. It was in his reign that the Third Estate, initially the burgesses, started to gain influence.

For the next 250 years this was to be the pattern of Scottish parliamentary government. Every so often, a strong Scottish king would bend the Parliament to his will. But between times, and for much longer periods, the country often lacked strong government.

The king or queen was often an infant who had inherited the throne after their parent's violent or untimely death. The Maid of Norway, for example, was only four when she was offered the throne, and both Mary, Queen of Scots and James VI were infant monarchs.

At these times of royal 'minority', the Parliament (or Three Estates) had a key role in appointing a **Guardian** or a **Regent**. It also had a role in removing them if they were no good, and in fighting off threats from over-ambitious members of the nobility. As a series of checks and balances, the system worked quite well.

Robert I, the Bruce, was a great king, but his successors didn't have an easy time. His son and heir, David II, succeeded to the throne in 1329, aged 5, and he was married to a girl of the same age! The Guardian of Scotland during much of David II's minority was Robert the Steward. As David's uncle, he was a rival for power. David II was nominally king of Scots for 42 years. Seven years were spent in France for his own safety and then eleven years as a prisoner in England. Does this sound suspicious? In fairness, the Scottish Parliament did a reasonable job of keeping Robert the Steward from becoming 'the wicked uncle'.

The seal of David II (1329–71). As *Rex Scotorum,* King of Scots, he endured a turbulent reign.

Declaration of Arbroath

The **Declaration of Arbroath** (1320) was a letter sent to the Pope by the barons of Scotland asserting Scotland's independence. It stated:

For as long as one hundred of us remain alive, we will never on any conditions submit to the domination of the English. It is not for glory nor riches, nor honours that we fight, but for freedom alone, which no good man gives up except with his life.

Robert the Bruce

- Find out about the tactics used at the Battle of Bannockburn.
- Why was the Scottish victory a historical turning point?
- What had Scotland gained?
- What caused the death of Robert the Bruce?
- How did James Douglas fulfil a vow to his king?
- Visit the **Robert the Bruce Trail** in Dumfries and Galloway. The trail sites tell the story of how a nobleman from south-west Scotland recovered the country's freedom.

  Look it up online at:
  www.brucetrust.co.uk/trail.html

King Robert I and his army, with the town of Stirling in the background.

Mary, Queen of Scots and the Reformation

In 1543, Mary was crowned Queen of Scots at the ripe old age of nine months.

Her cousin, James Hamilton, Earl of Arran, ruled in her place as Regent until 1554. Then Mary's mother, Queen Mary of Guise, widow of King James V, took control until her own death in 1560.

During this time, Mary was being raised at the French court, partly for her own safety. This was a strategy approved by Parliament shortly after her coronation. In the last year of her 13-year absence, when Mary was Queen of France, one of Scotland's most important Parliaments assembled. In 1560 this **'Reformation' Parliament** gathered in Edinburgh to legislate for the establishment of the Protestant Church and the abolition of Roman Catholicism.

The Protestant party in the Parliament was strong at this time. It was able to pass acts 'abolishing idolatry and the mass', as well as the powers of the Pope, stating 'the Bishop of Rome has no jurisdiction within this realm'. It also sanctioned the new **Confession of Faith**, prepared by John Calvin of Geneva. The Third Estate, allied

Queen of France

In 1558, aged only 15, Mary married Francis, Dauphin of France, at a glittering ceremony in Notre Dame Cathedral in Paris. Mary was Queen of France for only two and a half years when Francis died. She was left a young widow. In 1561, Mary returned to Scotland.

Fast fact

It is said that St Andrew felt unworthy to be crucified on the same kind of cross as Jesus. The flag of Scotland, called the **Saltire**, shows the type of cross used instead for Andrew's crucifixion.

There are three flagpoles outside the Scottish Parliament at Holyrood. Which flags are flown on them? Another two flagpoles are put up when needed – when the Queen, or the head of another country, visits.

with most of the nobility, had successfully outvoted the Catholic clergy.

As a good Catholic, Mary of Guise, the Regent, had refused to countersign these acts. Her daughter, on returning to Scotland from France, refused to sign them too. In 1567, Catholic clergy were excluded from the Parliament and the acts were finally passed – but only after the forced abdication of Mary, Queen of Scots. Her son James VI, aged just one, succeeded his mother on the Scottish throne. Now another infant monarch needed another set of Guardians.

Control within the government was hotly contested over this period. There was an uneasy mix of the Catholic pro-French party, Protestant pro-English, the crown and the nobility, the Parliament and the Convention of Royal Burghs, the General Assembly of the Church of Scotland, and the Privy Council. Then as now, rival bodies and factions had to learn to co-exist. Political alliances had to be built up and maintained. 'Coalition government' was the norm – not so different from the modern situation.

An 18th-century view of Parliament Square in Edinburgh.

Coalitions

- The United Kingdom had a **coalition** government during the Second World War, similar to the **Community of the Realm** in medieval Scotland.
- Take a look at current or recent coalition governments, such as the one at Westminster in 2010 between Conservatives and Liberal Democrats, or the 1999–2007 coalition at Holyrood between Labour and the Liberal Democrats. You might also consider the coalition of the European Parliaments in Brussels and Strasbourg. In what ways is a coalition government weaker or stronger than a one-party administration?

Why did Scotland lose its Parliament?

In 1604, soon after James VI of Scotland inherited the throne of England and went to London, he tried to unite the two Parliaments.

However the time wasn't ripe, and both Parliaments rejected his plans outright. For the time being, it was probably enough for the two countries to get used to sharing a monarch. A shared parliament could wait.

But only 100 years after the Union of the Crowns, both Parliaments voted in favour of a parliamentary union. The Scottish Parliament voted 110 in favour and 69 against the Union which was to create the United Kingdom of Great Britain. The two countries would have one Union Flag – the crosses of St Andrew and St George were to be joined.

'Mony a mickle maks a muckle ...'

William Paterson (a Scot) traded with the West Indies, founded the Bank of England in 1694 and the Bank of Scotland in 1695. The country's first bank was the only one ever founded by an Act of the Parliament of Scotland.

John Law, son of an Edinburgh goldsmith, founded the Banque de France in 1720.

Henry Duncan, a minister from Ruthwell in Dumfriesshire, founded the world's first savings bank in 1810.

Find out more about these gifted men.

And what does 'mony a mickle maks a muckle' mean?

Answer on page 40

Above: Brooch commemorating the Union of Scotland and England.

Left: Early 17th-century fan with symbols reflecting the Union of Scotland and England.

The Union of 1707

Scottish arguments against closer union	Scottish arguments for closer union
• We don't like being governed by the English. • Our culture will be impoverished by the loss of our own Parliament. • We've been made bankrupt by the **Darien Scheme** (see below) – English investors pulled out and we were left to surrender to Spain. • We're surrendering our independence.	• Just give us the money and we'll agree (English bribes to some Scottish nobles). • Our economy's fragile. We need access to English markets. • We want to join the British Empire, help to build it up, and share its benefits. • This will secure the Protestant succession of our monarch. We don't want a Catholic Jacobite succession.

Many Scots opposed the terms of the Union and felt betrayed. It was an 'end to an auld sang' that had lasted 500 years. Although Scotland was to keep her own laws, judges and form of worship. Mobs went on the rampage in many towns trying to track down traitors – the nobles who had accepted bribes. Martial law was declared.

The Darien Scheme

What was it? Why was it such a disaster for Scotland? And what does the German chest (below), with its complex locking system, have to do with the Scheme?

Answers on page 40

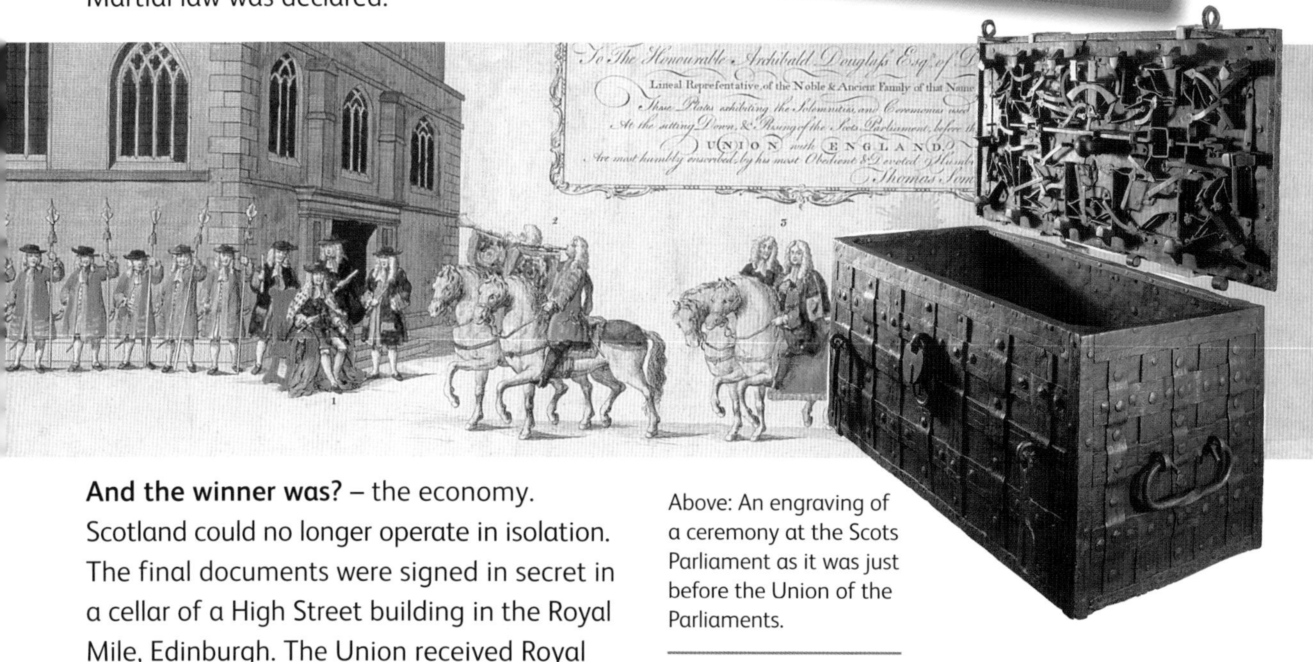

Above: An engraving of a ceremony at the Scots Parliament as it was just before the Union of the Parliaments.

And the winner was? – the economy. Scotland could no longer operate in isolation. The final documents were signed in secret in a cellar of a High Street building in the Royal Mile, Edinburgh. The Union received Royal Assent from Queen Anne on 6 March 1707.

Eighteenth-century flashpoints

Battles, taxes – and no more bagpipe music.

There was a mood change after the parliamentary Union, but few immediate effects. The Scottish Lords tried to scrap it in 1713, but were narrowly defeated. When Queen Anne, the last Stuart monarch, died, leaving no direct heir, there was a small Jacobite uprising in support of the Old Pretender – James Stuart, son of King James VII. Scots Lords with Jacobite sympathies ended up in the Tower of London and a few were executed.

An English tax system was now forced on the Scots. A malt tax was levied on brewing and distilling, leading to riots. Heavy taxes on tea, wines and spirits led to smuggling on a national scale. When a smuggler was hanged, it was no surprise when a rioting mob lynched a captain of the Edinburgh City Guard and hanged him in retaliation.

Following the Battle of Culloden, the failure of the 1745 Jacobite Rising led to the banning of weapons, Highland dress, and bagpipe music. Strategically placed Highland forts and garrisons, manned by the British army, kept the Highlanders in check.

Above: A Lochaber axe, as carried by the Edinburgh City Guard.

The Porteous Riots

On 14 April 1736 Andrew Wilson, an Edinburgh merchant, was hanged for robbing a customhouse. As he was cut down, a few in the sympathetic crowd threw stones at the hangman. Captain John Porteous of the Edinburgh City Guard ordered his men to fire into the crowd, killing several people. Those who had lost friends and servants demanded justice. Porteous was tried, condemned, pardoned and ultimately lynched for his actions.

Prisoners were executed, or transported to plantations in the West Indies. The clan system was destroyed.

It took until the 1750s before peace led to an upturn in industry. Toiling on the land was being replaced by more and bigger factories. People were on the move to try to improve their quality of life. The British Linen Company gave loans to linen manufacturers. Glasgow became the biggest British port to import tobacco. There was also a first Scottish prime minister – John Stuart, the Earl of Bute.

By the 1780s, Robert Burns was becoming Scotland's national poet, and he never failed to notice any foibles of the government. His radical political views were read eagerly, and soon copies of Burns' *Poems* (1786) joined the Bible in the home of every educated Scot. The New Town and the leaders of the **Enlightenment** transformed Edinburgh. In turn, Adam Smith's *Wealth of Nations* (1776) transformed ideas about commerce and free trade. But after the Clearances began in the Highlands, where tenant crofters were replaced by sheep, it was felt that Scotland was losing its identity. It had become North Britain. No one was promoting Scotland in the House of Commons – and, to add to Scots' woes, in 1799 income tax was introduced.

John Stuart Third Earl of Bute

Robert Burns

Adam Smith

Read more about ...

It was said that 'twelve highlanders and a bagpipe make a rebellion'. Eviction from the Highlands led to a better life for some, but it changed the Highland landscape forever.

Far right: A late 18th-century tobacco shop sign.
Background: Plans of the New Town of Edinburgh by James Craig.

The Westminster Parliament up to 1939

At last – '*We're a' Jock Tamson's bairns.*'

The colours on this brooch are very important to the wearer. This brooch has purple, green and white stones – the colours of a supporter of the suffragette movement.

It was a long haul for every eligible Briton to get the vote. The Great War (1914–1918) helped the breakthrough – especially for women, who suddenly had to do work traditionally done by men. In 1918 the vote was given to all women over 30 and men over 21.

By 1900 Westminster was well represented by Scots 'at the helm'. New political parties were also headed up by Scots, such as James Keir Hardie, in 1892 the first Labour MP. It took up to the onset of the Second World War before Scotland reclaimed more parliamentary powers from Westminster. Why did it take so long? Read the Timeline opposite to identify the major events which led to social upheaval.

Prime Ministers

Scotland has supplied many British prime ministers at Westminster. Find out which prime ministers since 1902 were born in Scotland. For help and information, visit:

www.able2know.org/topic/97637-1

'Bonny fechters'

Flora Drummond

Flora Drummond (1878–1949) from Arran was drawn into the suffragette movement. She became a militant leader of the Women's Social and Political Union and tried to 'lobby' the Prime Minister, Henry Campbell-Bannerman – a Glaswegian.

Unsuccessful, she had two suffragette women stamped, labelled and posted to 10 Downing Street! Imprisoned nine times for her perseverance, she was known as 'The General'.

Elsie Maud Inglis

Against all odds, Elsie Maud Inglis (1864–1917) qualified as a surgeon and founded her own maternity hospital, staffed solely by women. She helped to establish the suffragette movement in Scotland.

Timeline

1822 George IV visits Scotland, the first by a British monarch since 1651. Stage-managed by Sir Walter Scott, tartan and bagpipe music are back in vogue.

1832 First Reform Act gives the right to vote to those who own or rent property. Before this, only one in every 125 adult Scots had voting rights.

1837 Start of Queen Victoria's reign.

1846 Highland famine – potato crops fail because of a deadly fungus.

1850 Almost half of Scots live in towns and cities, leading to poor housing and health problems. Glasgow doubles in population within 50 years.

1867 Most householders over 21 years are given vote – except women!

1868 Second Reform Act extends the vote to skilled workers. Scotland gets seven extra parliamentary seats at Westminster.

1884 Third Reform Act gives all male house owners the right to vote. Two out of three men can now vote.

1885 The Scottish Office is established in London as a government department with a Secretary for Scotland.

1892 James Keir Hardie becomes the first Labour MP. He was a supporter of votes for women.

1893 First women graduate from Scottish universities (before Oxford and Cambridge universities).

1901 Two-thirds of Scots now live in the Central Belt. Queen Victoria dies.

1905 Scots rule at Westminster. Henry Campbell-Bannerman succeeds fellow Scot, Arthur Balfour, as Prime Minister.

1911 Ramsay McDonald becomes leader of the Labour Party and first Labour Prime Minister in 1924.

1913 Bill for Scottish Home Rule is passed. It is halted by the First World War.

1914 War is declared. Women take on men's work as soldiers flock to the Front.

1915 Rent Strike in Glasgow as landlords force up rents.

1918 Women over 30 are given the vote. All men over 21 get the vote.

1924 First Labour Government elected. Ramsay McDonald becomes Prime Minister. Red Clydesider Jimmy Maxton states: 'Give us our Parliament in Scotland!'

1926 The post of Secretary for Scotland becomes Secretary of State for Scotland, with a seat in cabinet.

1928 Universal suffrage is granted. All people over 21 now have the right to vote.

1934 The Scottish National Party is formed.

1939 St Andrew's House, the headquarters of the Scottish Office, opens in Edinburgh.

Travelling the distance

If you visit Holyrood, look out for the artwork featuring 100 handwritten sentences from women around Scotland, about their female role models.

A number of women went to prison in their attempt to secure the vote for women. On her release from Holloway Prison, suffragette Mary Phillips was met by her friends who laid on an impressive event – with tartan and bagpipes. Mary Phillips served three months from June to September 1908.

What is devolution?

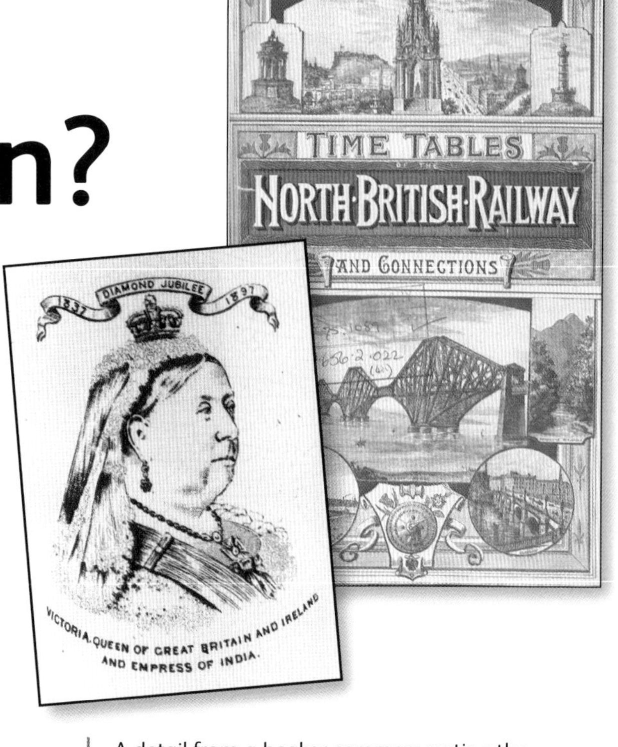

A detail from a beaker commemorating the Diamond Jubilee of 'Victoria, Queen of Great Britain and Ireland and Empress of India' and a timetable for the North British Railway. Scotland was often referred to as North Britain in heavy industries such as manufacturing and rail.

Devolution is a process. It may be seen as government delegated from the top down to the grass roots – that is, government closer to the people.

In the case of Scotland, government has been redirected away from the House of Commons at Westminster to the Scottish Parliament at Holyrood. Devolution is best understood by comparing it with the more centralised, imperial government that came before it.

In the 19th century, big European countries, such as the United Kingdom, France or Spain, crushed the idea of 'local' cultures in favour of a single national ruling culture – British, French, Spanish. Under Queen Victoria, those living in different parts of the British Isles were almost all proud to be British first and Scottish, Irish or Welsh second. The British Empire was also Scotland's, and Scotland's world outlook was thus imperial.

The British Parliament at Westminster once governed not just the whole British Isles, but also (via the Colonial Office) vast areas of Asia, Africa, the Pacific, the Americas, and so on. Scotland's entire national effort was in the direction of colonisation – Britain was the most successful colonising country in history.

Quick question

A question to ponder?
Do you think in the future Scotland, Wales and Northern Ireland are likely to want more devolution? Or will they wish to keep the current arrangements?

See page 40

Devolved matters

Devolved matters in Scotland include at present:	Reserved matters retained by Westminster:
• Farming, forestry, fishing	• The UK economy
• Education, training, social work, health	• Taxation
• Housing, industry and enterprise, the environment	• International trade
• Transport, local government, police and fire services	• Defence
• Justice and Scots legal system	• Consumer affairs
• Representation of Scotland in the EU	• Social security and the benefit system
• Music, theatre and culture	• Representation of the UK in the EU
	• Child Support Agency
	• National Lottery and gambling

The Scotland Act of 2012 transferred further powers, some of which are:

- New borrowing powers in the Scottish Budget
- Power to create new taxes
- Role of the Crown Estate

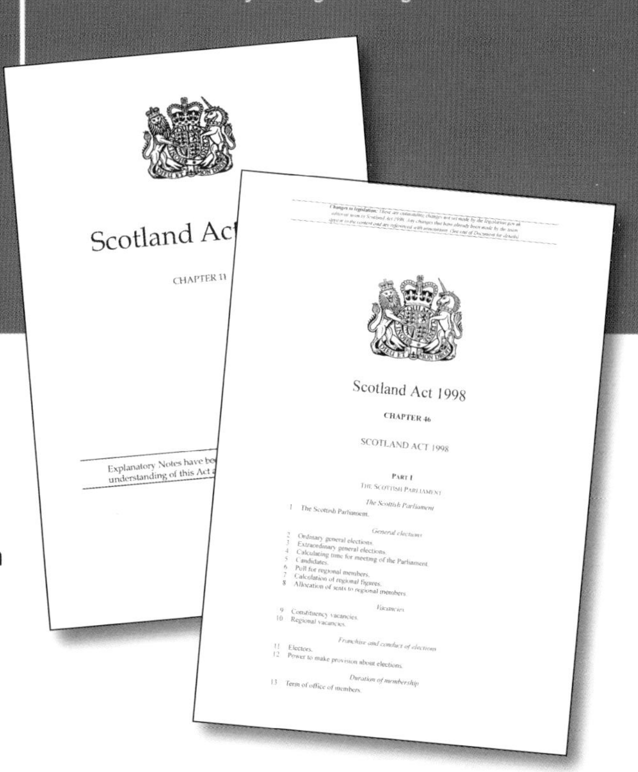

Scotland Act

CHAPTER 11

Scotland Act 1998

CHAPTER 46

SCOTLAND ACT 1998

PART I

THE SCOTTISH PARLIAMENT

The Scottish Parliament

1 The Scottish Parliament.

General elections

2 Ordinary general elections.
3 Extraordinary general elections.
4 Calculating time for meeting of the Parliament.
5 Candidates.
6 Poll for regional members.
7 Calculation of regional figures.
8 Allocation of seats to regional members.

Vacancies

9 Constituency vacancies.
10 Regional vacancies.

Franchise and conduct of elections

11 Electors.
12 Power to make provision about elections.

Duration of membership

13 Term of office of members.

Today, Europe's various empires (British, French, Russian, Spanish, Dutch, German, Belgian and Italian) have almost all gone, and the United Kingdom's overseas empire has been transformed into a Commonwealth of independent states. The home nations of Scotland and Wales have devolution – their own legislatures.

One part of the United Kingdom preferred its own independence. In 1921, Ireland opted to split in two, and the larger part, the Republic of Ireland, left not just the United Kingdom but also in due course made its exit from the British Commonwealth. Meanwhile, Northern Ireland voted to remain British and, like Scotland and Wales, it has a devolved government. The range of matters devolved from Westminster varies among the three minority home nations.

Stepping stones to devolution

Tak tent o tyme or tyme be tint.
[Time and tide wait for no man.]
Traditional saying

Food and motor fuel ration books, and a coupon for two units of power after the Second World War.

It was a long road to restoring the Scottish Parliament. The Second World War had left the United Kingdom's economy severely weakened. There was high unemployment, and basic goods were scarce, with ration coupons still in use in the 1950s.

But political change was afoot. By 1945 the first Scottish National Party member was briefly elected at Westminster. By 1950 a convention was formed to campaign for devolution. Over one and a quarter million Scots signed a covenant, demanding their own Scottish Parliament. However, a little more patience would be required!

In the 1960s, there was a revival of the Scottish National Party, with Winnie Ewing winning the Hamilton by-election in 1967.

A major stepping stone in 1971 was the Upper Clyde Shipbuilders work-in. As the yards were threatened with closure, the ship-builders locked themselves in to continue working. They saved the yards, and their livelihood, as Westminster eventually relented.

1967: Winnie Ewing campaigns for – and wins – a seat at Westminster. • 1975: North Sea oil.

Think about it ...

In 2009, the Scottish Parliament passed an Act aiming for Scotland to get all of its own energy from renewable sources by 2025. What range of renewables does Scotland have? Think about ways in which we can all conserve energy?

Answers on page 40

Then, in 1975, for the first time precious North Sea oil was pumped ashore in Scotland. Did Scotland believe in itself again?

Fast fact

The main vigil for the Scottish Parliament was set up on Calton Hill in Edinburgh after the General Election of 1992. It remained there for 1980 days!

Not quite! Supporters' hopes were dashed in 1979 with the first devolution referendum. It failed to get the result needed. The verdict? One third wanted it, one third didn't, one third didn't care. Ten years later, another convention campaigned for devolution, meeting in the Assembly Hall, Edinburgh. It took, however, until 1997, when a General Election at Westminster brought New Labour to power, and then the second home-rule referendum was held.

This time the result was 75/25 in favour of a Scottish Parliament. By the following year the Scotland Act declared, 'There shall be a Scottish Parliament' – these words are inscribed forever in its new home at Holyrood. They appear on the Mace (see page 19).

1997: Scotland's choice. • 2011: By now wind turbines are a familiar sight throughout Scotland.

Opening of the Scottish Parliament

1 July 1999

The Queen with Donald Dewar (above, left) and David Steel (right) at the opening of Scotland's Parliament in July 1999, and a procession of children celebrating the occasion (below).

The scene was set. Hundreds of cheering schoolchildren and tourists lined Edinburgh's Royal Mile. It was the stert o a new sang.

Flags waved, and Concorde, flanked by the Red Arrows, flew past majestically. There was a deafening gun salute from the Castle. The great and the good joined the long procession of the new 129 Members of the Scottish Parliament (MSPs) making their way from Parliament House up the Lawnmarket to their temporary home.

The new devolved Scottish Parliament met in the Assembly Hall of the Church of Scotland on the Mound, and it was formally opened by Her Majesty the Queen. Fanfares greeted her arrival from the Palace of Holyrood as she alighted from an open horse-drawn landau.

The Queen presented a silver mace, inscribed with the opening line of the Scotland Act 1998: 'There shall be a Scottish Parliament.' This showed that the Queen had passed law-making powers to the people and their Parliament. Four timeless values are engraved on the mace: Compassion, Integrity, Justice and Wisdom.

The Mace

The Mace is made from silver with an inlaid band of gold panned from Scottish rivers. The band symbolises the marriage between the Parliament, the people and the land.

This historic presentation was followed by the Robert Burns song 'A Man's a Man for a' that', sung unaccompanied by Sheena Wellington, a Scottish folk singer. The song was written in 1795 at the height of the French Revolution. The First Minister Donald Dewar talked of Burns in his opening speech.

There were many memorable parts. It was, as Donald Dewar said, 'a moment anchored in our history'. Scotland had its own Parliament again after a lapse of 293 years. Listen to Donald Dewar's speech at **'Parliament TV'** on the website of the Scottish Parliament.

Donald Dewar
(1937–2000)

Often called 'the Father of the Nation', Donald Dewar was a great fighter for the revival of the Scottish Parliament. A brilliant speaker, Dewar was elected First Minister in 1999, but died suddenly in the year 2000. He had commissioned the new Parliament building at Holyrood, but sadly did not see it finished.

Dr Winnie Ewing

At the first meeting on 12 May, 1999, Dr Winnie Ewing, Mother of the House, quietly reopened the new politics of Scotland with the words:

'The Scottish Parliament, adjourned on 25th March 1707, is hereby reconvened.'

Parliament plans its new home

Enric Miralles and Donald Dewar discuss the model for the new Parliament building.

Set a stoot hert to a stey brae.
[It takes a stout heart to climb a steep hill.] Traditional saying

By the end of the 20th century, it was clear that Scotland would need a purpose-built complex to house its Parliament. Architect Enric Miralles from Barcelona won the competition held in 1998 to create an inspirational workplace for MSPs and their staff. It would be designed as a national symbol or icon. The architect, in partnership with a team from RMJM (Robert Matthew Johnson Marshall) in Edinburgh, created just that at the chosen site of an old brewery opposite Holyroodhouse.

The work began in 2000, with the superstructure completed in early 2001. Tragically Miralles died in 2000, but his vision was sustained by his widow, also an architect. The site itself was challenging. It faced an ancient royal palace in the most historic part of the city – and it was tucked below the small mountain of Arthur's Seat, one of Edinburgh's extinct volcanoes. How was the Parliament to merge with the cityscape and landscape, or complement it?

By design

The shape of the saltire, slightly tilted, is embedded in the smooth concrete. The 'Skating Minister' (the Reverend Robert Walker, right), painted by Sir Henry Raeburn, is also used as a stylised shape. Even the crow-stepped gable design, common in older Scottish domestic architecture, is flipped around and placed under the windows of the MSPs' offices. When the first office workers moved in on 2 August 2004, they marvelled at the detail and vision of the overall design.

Eco-friendly by design

Beer had been brewed in this part of Edinburgh for over 1000 years. By 1900 there were 17 breweries around Holyrood, using the natural springs. The best known of the Holyrood wells were the Wells o' Wearie – deep pools under Samson's Ribs, on Arthur's Seat. Many other wells were found under the site of the Debating Chamber. ('The Bonnie Wells o' Wearie' is a famous traditional song title.)

Although no longer safe for drinking, spring water from the old brewery cools the Parliament building, and is used for the toilets. Stone from the brewery site was re-used and packed into *gabions* (strong metal cages). These now form outside walls in parts of the complex.

Miralles and the designers used visual symbols to represent Scotland in the new building's design. Roofs in the shape of upturned boats, the Debating Chamber with its massive oak beams, the 'concrete branch-es' with grassy tops reaching out into the parkland beyond – all of these details help the complex to 'sit within the land'.

Below: The scene of a crowded Holyrood Park, looking back over the city to the Castle, with Calton Hill and Nelson's Monument on the right. The scene has changed very little today from the time of Queen Victoria, whose visit to Edinburgh in 1881 is commemorated here.

Say but little ...

Abair ach beagan is abair gu math e
[Say but little and say it well]

Queensberry House and the Garden Lobby.

One of the Gaelic text panels set into the Canongate Wall of the Parliament perhaps serves as a reminder to the MSPs. Humour, imagination, poetry and style are abundant on this site. The Parliament had much to squeeze into the limited space – a debating chamber, committee rooms, MSPs' offices and administrative services, yet it still had to feel like a 'gathering place' and to 'reflect the land' (Enric Miralles).

The oldest part of the site is Queensberry House (1667), in the Canongate. The once-grand town house was restored from its past as a barracks, a refuge and a hospital. To meet 21st-century needs, timber floors were replaced by concrete and steel, walls were strengthened and windows made blast-proof. Under its red pantiled roof are the rooms for the Presiding Officer and other staff, as well as the Dewar Room housing a library of the very first First Minister's books.

An upturned boat now in use as a fisherman's shed.

Today the old kitchen garden of Queensberry House is the Garden Lobby, covered by leaf-shaped roof lights (now a favourite spot for TV interviews). The iconic roof-lines of the complex are viewed best if you climb the Radical Road on Arthur's Seat. From above you'll see the four towers that house the Committee Rooms – 'like boats in a harbour'. Think of upturned keels, when boats are hauled up in winter – that's the vision the architect wanted.

The Scottish Parliament buildings with Queensberry House and the surrounding landscape.

You can also appreciate the landscaping of the site as you look down from the hill. Trees in the grounds, native wildflowers and grassy extensions from the buildings blend into the backdrop of Holyrood Park.

Fast facts

- In the first 9 weeks of the Scottish Parliament building being open to the public, there were 100,000 visitors.
- On the opening day there was a 'Riding' (or procession) of people from every constituency in Scotland. They walked down the Royal Mile from the old Parliament Hall behind St Giles, to Holyrood. This marked the age-old tradition of Parliament and people working in partnership.
- A rowan tree (*caorann* in Gaelic) was planted on the Canongate site. It was thought to be a magical tree. If planted outside your door, it was meant to protect you from evil or enchantment.

ABAIR ACH BEAGAN IS ABAIR GU MATH E.

Say but little and say it well

PROVERB

Left: Proverb from the Canongate Wall, which you can see on page 26.

Think about it ...

How would you describe democracy? Think of some of the rights and responsibilities of a citizen in a democracy. Find out a little about the European Court of Human Rights.

See page 40

Below: The 1685 Riding of Parliament.

Open the doors!

9 October 2004

'A landmark for 21st-century democracy ...'

Her Majesty The Queen

Above: Her Majesty The Queen is shown around the new Parliament building on the official opening day, Saturday 9 October 2004.

Another stirring ceremony heralded the official opening of the Parliament building at Holyrood by Her Majesty The Queen. Read the first two parts of Edwin Morgan's poem (page 39), spoken on the day by Liz Lochhead. It paints a wonderful word picture of the unique building. 'Is it not a mystery?'

The poet invites the listeners to venture down the Royal Mile with him. He reassures his audience of the choice of location, selected by Donald Dewar. Finally, Edwin Morgan asks, 'What do the people want of the place?' He speaks directly to the people who govern us.

It is to be 'no nest of fearties,' he says, and ends with a warning to the MSPs: 'We give you this great building, don't let your work and hope be other than great when you enter and begin.' Turn to page 39 to read more of this inspiring poem by Scotland's Makar (national poet) or Poet Laureate of the day, Edwin Morgan (1920–2010).

Scotland's writers

- *'Scotland is indefinable; it has no unity except upon the map.'* This is a neat description by **Robert Louis Stevenson** (1850–94). Stevenson was not a politician, but a writer. Scottish writers, playwrights and poets can tune us into the past, but they can also try to forecast what people and the country want for the future.
- Study the **Canongate Wall** with its quotes from some Scottish writers. Make a note of a few of your favourite quotes. What do you specially like about them?
- The Scottish Parliament's first Writer in Residence, James Robertson, wrote eleven fine sonnets about the new Parliament.

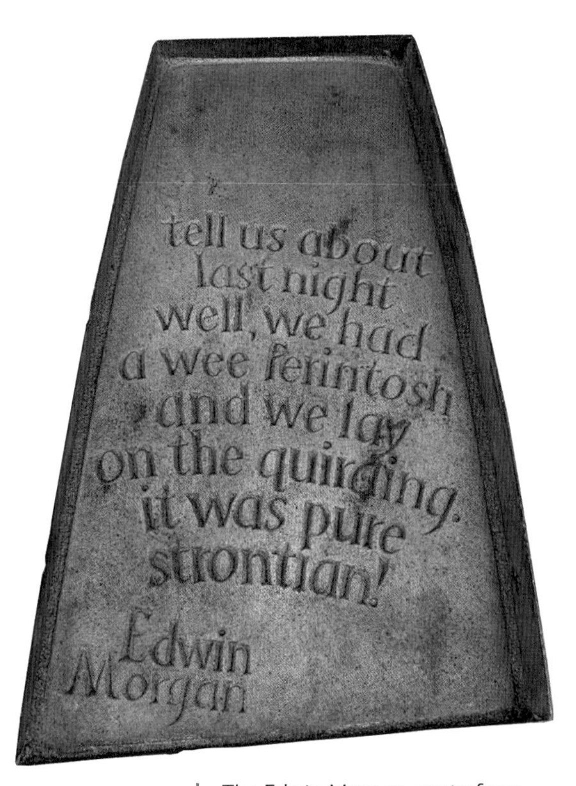

The Edwin Morgan quote from the Canongate Wall, which you can see on page 26.

At the Royal opening in 1999, the new Parliament was gifted a mace by the Queen. In 2004 a new sculpture, 'Honours of Scotland', was presented, as a reminder of Scotland's Crown Jewels – the Crown, the Sword and the Sceptre (also known as the Honours of Scotland). The original three Honours of Scotland were always on display when the old Parliament met. You can see them today in Edinburgh Castle.

Download ...

a commemorative programme at:

www.scottish.parliament.uk/VisitorInformation/Programme.pdf

Honours of Scotland

The Three Honours sculpture (below) was commissioned by the Incorporation of Goldsmiths of the City of Edinburgh and presented by Her Majesty The Queen to the Scottish Parliament on the opening of Holyrood.

The Scottish Parliament
Pàrlamaid na h-Alba

Brisidh an teanga bhog an cneath. [A soft tongue will blunt wrath.] Biblical proverb

As can be seen from the Canongate Wall, texts in Scots, Gaelic and English are all represented. There has always been linguistic diversity in Scotland. King James IV had a great gift for languages, including Gaelic. The Scottish Parliament gives equal respect to both English and Gaelic (as stated in The Gaelic Language Act, 2005). For historical reasons, it also recognises the use of Scots. British Sign Language (BSL) used for the deaf is recognised too.

English is used as the working language of the Debating Chamber and in legislation. However, to give equal opportunity to those non-fluent in English, anyone officially invited to address Parliament may do so in any language (if interpreters are arranged in advance). If you visit Holyrood's main lobby, you will see the visitors' guides in at least ten languages. The Parliament tries at all times to be open and accessible, and to allow people to engage with it.

Canongate Wall

There are many famous quotes and proverbs carved into stones on the Canongate Wall, including those shown on pages 23 and 25.

James IV (above) was well educated and a fluent polyglot (he spoke or wrote in many languages). In 1498 a Spanish envoy reported that, 'his knowledge of languages is wonderful. He is well read in the Bible. He has read many Latin and French histories and profited by them.'

Public Gallery seating in the Debating Chamber.

The Parliament runs sessions in schools across Scotland, as well as welcoming young people to Holyrood. The Committees can also go out on fact-finding visits or conduct their meetings outside Edinburgh.

But how does the Scottish Parliament actually work? Well, the easiest way to answer that question is by making a visit to the splendid Debating Chamber.

Read all about it ...

The Scottish Parliament as early as the 16th century made it a law that there would be a school in every parish. This was to encourage children to read their Bible.

Time for Reflection

Each week, before Parliamentary Business begins, an invited speaker addresses the MSPs, often on a topical issue. Speakers come from across the spectrum of religious beliefs, and some do not represent any particular faith. As with the Parliament's language policy, **Time for Reflection** provides for the country's diversity.

The Debating Chamber

The loodest bummer's no the best bee. Scots saying

Nicola Sturgeon, MSP, speaking in the Debating Chamber.

At the heart of the new Parliament is the Debating Chamber, directly above the Main Hall. A soaring lattice of oak beams supports the roof. These roof timbers echo the 17th-century hammer-beam roof of the old Parliament Hall on the Royal Mile (see below).

James Robertson, the Parliament's Writer in Residence, wrote: 'Under the massive beams and banks of lights, the oak and sycamore's pale, weeping grace gives a grove-like quality to the place' (2004).

The semi-circular shape of the Chamber is designed to be very different from the Chamber of the House of Commons at Westminster. Miralles and his team spent months getting it just right. The arc shape is chosen to discourage confrontation.

Old Parliament Hall

The impressive stained-glass window and hammer-beam roof of the Great Hall of the old Parliament House in Parliament Square, Edinburgh.

The Westminster design was initially intended to keep the two parties, Whig and Tory, two sword-lengths apart from each other. At Holyrood this tradition has been abandoned.

Meetings of the full Parliament are held in the Chamber, where each week the 129 MSPs have their debates and attend First Minister's Question Time. This is where Scotland's laws are debated and voted upon.

Part of the Presiding Officer's role is to divide up the time and allow as many MSPs as possible to contribute. Each MSP's desk has a lectern, microphone and voting console. The electronic console identifies each speaker. Preparation of new laws is carried out in the Committee Rooms – the engine rooms of the Parliament.

The layout of the Chamber at Holyrood encourages the MSPs to raise the quality of their debates. From a raised seat in the central area of the curved Chamber, the Presiding Officer ensures rules are kept. The Public Gallery gives a view of all proceedings from above.

Debating techniques

What do you think 'the loodest bummer's no the best bee' actually means? How would you prepare for an important debate?

Suggestions on page 40

Look, listen, take part!

Look, listen – or take part, if you can! The Public Gallery is purpose-built for use by the public and the media. Debates and meetings can be followed live on the internet. And of course you can visit in person. Phone Visitor Services or e-mail if you wish to attend a debate.

New Debating Chamber

Voting systems

Elections to the Scottish Parliament are held every four years, and each voter has two votes.

The first Government was a Labour-Liberal Democrat alliance elected in 1999, as was the second in 2003; the third elected a SNP minority government in 2007, and the fourth in 2011 also returned a SNP government – this time with an outright majority. Currently, the Scottish Parliament is made up of 129 democratically elected MSPs.

There are two kinds of MSP – 73 **constituency members** represent 73 individual geographical areas and their electorates; and 56 **regional members** (or **list** MSPs) are elected for 8 larger regions, with each region returning 7 MSPs (see map opposite).

The 73 constituency members are elected by the **First Past the Post** (**FPP**) system. This method of election is often compared to a horse race. Only the winner is elected, and all the runners-up are discarded. The 'also-rans' may have been pipped at the post by a whisker – less than 50 or 100 votes in a total count of 30,000. Re-counts are therefore not uncommon. But the FPP system fails to take account of how **everyone** voted, especially in the case of minority parties and independents.

This is where the other system comes in useful. The **Additional Member System** (**AMS**) method is used for electing the 56 regional MSPs. Under this system the entire regional vote is added up: seven winners are elected and this combines to produce a more widely spread result for each region.

It is thought that, between the two systems of voting, a much fairer and more accurate overall picture of the electorate's views is obtained.

Current Holyrood party representation includes the Scottish National Party (SNP), Labour, Conservative and the Liberal Democrat constituency MSPs; the same parties plus an Independent and two Greens also feature in the regional lists.

VOTE

BALLOT BOX

Other parties to have returned regional MSPs in the past include the Scottish Socialist Party, Scottish Senior Citizens' Unity Party, Save Stobhill Hospital, and Solidarity.

Party representation (in the 2011 Parliament) is SNP 67 seats, Labour 37 seats, Conservative 15 seats, Liberal Democrat 5, Independent 2 and Green 2.

In 2011 a total of 31 parties stood for election. Nineteen parties gained more than 1000 votes, 8 of these gained more than 20,000 votes, and only 4 gained more than 100,000 votes. Many small parties were 'single-issue' groupings, like Action to Save St John's Hospital, Scotland Against Crooked Lawyers, and the Anti-Trident Party. Some parties only stood in a single constituency.

Pulling in the votes

Find out about your own Holyrood constituency. Is there a good issue that might attract support from a wide range of voters? Think of topics like local job opportunities, sporting facilities, and so on.

See page 40

Right:
These 8 Holyrood parliamentary regions* each return 7 MSPs by AMS.

1 Central Scotland
2 Glasgow
3 Highlands and Islands
4 Lothian
5 Mid Scotland and Fife
6 North East Scotland
7 South Scotland
8 West Scotland

*As per the first periodic Review of Scottish Parliament Boundaries, which came into effect on 5 May 2011.

With COLONEL DUKE'S Compliments.

The Unionist Candidate for the Stirling Burghs.

SUPPORT THE UNIONIST.

HOW TO VOTE.

Supporters of **Colonel O. T. Duke** are respectfully requested to mark their BALLOT PAPER as under:—

1	BANNERMAN (Rt. Hon. Henry Campbell-Bannerman, G.C.B., 6 Grosvenor Place, London, S.W.)	
2	DUKE (Olliver Thomas Duke, United Service Club, Pall Mall, London.)	X

Printed and Published by James Hogg & Co., 5 King Street, Stirling.

Left: A Westminster election campaign leaflet issued by the Unionist candidate for the Burgh of Stirling, *c.*1895–1906.

Government and the Scottish Parliament

Which people make up the Scottish Parliament?

The largest party in the Scottish Parliament forms the Government. The Government is led by the First Minister, Cabinet Secretaries, Junior Ministers and Law Officers. The public may attend their discussions in the Debating Chamber at Holyrood.

Gangs its ain gait ...

The Scottish Parliament 'goes its own way' with titles not used in the UK Parliament:

First Minister = Prime Minister
Presiding Officer = Speaker
MSPs = Members of the Scottish Parliament, responsible to the people of Scotland, who hold the Scottish Government to account.

How are new laws made?

The Parliament discusses and scrutinises the Scottish Government's plans and policies through its various committees.

Each committee has a remit to cover a special topic – such as Education, Health, or Transport. The committees are made up of a group of MSPs from the different parties.

A Bill is introduced in Parliament at the start of the process (**Stage 1**). After the policy has been studied carefully in committee, it is written up in the form of a Committee Report (**Stage 2**). Once a plan has been developed to this stage – that is, to the satisfaction of its committee – it is discussed in the Debating Chamber by the full Parliament of MSPs. Parliament then votes to accept, amend or reject the Bill (**Stage 3**).

The Scottish Parliament.

If Parliament approves the Bill, it goes to the Queen for the Royal Assent. After the Queen has signed it, the Bill becomes law as an Act of Parliament.

And the detail?

That is the process of the legislation; but behind the scenes, much equally important work goes on along the way. Every Act of Parliament has wide-ranging legal implications, so its scope and wording requires careful advice from the Parliament's lawyers. And as well as being written by experts on the topic, a Bill also needs to be looked at by specialists. The Government will consult on its ideas and the Parliament will invite people to write in, or come in, to discuss the topics with the committees. So doctors and dentists might be asked about a health matter or teachers and lecturers on education topics. And so on.

Much of the Scottish Government's background work takes place in their offices in Edinburgh – such as St Andrew's House and Victoria Quay – and around Scotland, as well as in government departments and specialist agencies throughout the country. The government jigsaw in a modern state is a complex one.

Find out more ...

On the **Scottish Parliament website** click on 'Visit & Learn' for:

- Calendar of Events
- Education
- Environment and Sustainability
- Events and Exhibitions
- Explore Parliament
- History
- How the Parliament Works
- Leaflets and Guides
- Visiting the Parliament

Making cuts – less is more!

There is a worry that government is becoming too complex – and expensive – and may need pruning from time to time. If you had to make savings in government expenditure, what would you suggest cutting?

This is not an easy question. You'll need some time to answer it! It's a matter of *priorities*. Different political parties tend to have different answers to this sort of question.

See page 40

Victoria Quay in Leith, Edinburgh, is the largest home of the Scottish Government, with over 2000 civil servants.

Work and workplace

What is it like to work as an MSP in the Parliament?

The MSP Building has a unique façade of canted windows – in a shape inspired by the Skating Minister portrait (see page 20). Each office is built around a concrete frame (cast on the Holyrood site). Most of the upper windows have an oak lattice outside. The inside office accommodation has a window space for 'contemplation' and is often described as a 'monastic cell' – but it's a comfortable 21st-century version!

Somewhere near where you live is your local MSP's office. He/she represents the people in your constituency and will deal with local issues. Regional MSPs also have local offices. When the Parliament is in session, a MSP will usually be at Holyrood from Tuesday to Thursday to attend Parliamentary debates, work with other MSPs, raise questions with Scottish Government ministers – and work in committees.

In Holyrood's Tower Buildings there are six committee rooms. The rooms are beautifully designed, all with flowing lines and some windows acting as pictures, framing the parkland beyond.

Each committee is made up of between 5 to 15 MSPs from different parties. **Mandatory committees** look at such areas as Procedures, Appointments and Code of Conduct, Equal Opportunities, and Europe. **Subject committees** deal with areas such as Education, Health or Rural Development. These committees can set up enquiries and propose Bills, as well as examine Bills closely before they become new laws.

MSPs need to do their homework to be prepared for their busy roles. They attend Question Time in the Chamber when they can ask the First Minister or other Government ministers about the hot topics of the day. In the Chamber, members also discuss ideas for Bills and vote on them and all the other topics they have discussed.

Committee Room II in the Scottish Parliament.

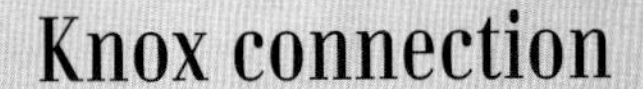

Knox connection

Look again!

The MSPs' windows jut out from the line of the wall. It's said that the architect Miralles developed this idea from the John Knox House in the Royal Mile (below). This is a building out of alignment with that part of the streetscape.

Detective trail

Who is your Constituency MSP?

Where is their surgery (office)? Your local library will have this information – or go to the Scottish Parliament website, find the 'MSPs' page, and click on the region of Scotland where you live on the map shown.

Which political party do they represent? Are they on any of the cross-party committees?

The interior of a MSP's office and the exterior (above), showing the canted windows.

Achievements of the first decade

This list is only a selection of Acts passed between the years 2000 and 2010. There are many more – but each with the purpose of improving standards and fairness, as well as the quality of life. As you look at the list, look at the range of interests – from those of young people to older ones, health, education, language, justice and transport. Each of the **devolved** areas is represented.

A Abolition of Poindings and Warrant Sales Act (2001)

B Budget Acts (2000–2010)

C Convention Rights Act (2001); Criminal Procedure Act (2004); Crofting Reform Act (2007); Climate Change Acts (2009 and 2010)

D Dog Fouling Act (2003); Disabled Persons' Parking Places Act (2009)

E Ethical Standards in Public Life Act (2000); Education: Additional Support for Learning Act (2004); Edinburgh Tramline Act (2006)

F Feudal Tenure Act abolished (2000); Freedom of Information Act (2002); Fur Farming Act (2002); Flood Risk Management Act (2009)

G Gaelic Language Act (2005); Glasgow Commonwealth Games Act (2008)

H Housing Act (2001); Homelessness Act (2003); Human Issues Act (2006)

L Land Reform Act (2003)

M Medical Services Act (2004); Marine: Health of Scottish Marine Areas Act (2010)

N National Parks Act (2000); Nature Conservation Act (2004)

P Public Finance and Accountability Act (2000); Protection of Wild Mammals Act (2002); Protection of Children Act (2003); Planning Act (2006); Public Health Act (2006)

R Regulation of Care Act (2001)

S Standards in Scottish Schools Act (2000); Salmon Conservation Act (2001); Scottish Outdoor Access Code Act (2003); Smoking, Health and Social Care Act (2005)

T Transport Act (2001); Tenements Act (2004); Tourist Boards Act (2006)

V Vulnerable Witnesses Act (2004)

W Water Industry Act (2002); Water Environment and Services Act (2003); Waverley Railway Act (2006)

Can you find out more?

The post of Commissioner for Young People was created by an Act passed in 2003. Who is the present holder of the post? What work do they carry out? Which Acts passed by the Parliament have affected you in some way?

Mystery object

Find out what this object is and what it commemorates.

Answer on page 40

Tenth Birthday Party!

A special birthday party for 143 10-year-old children was held on 1 July 2009 to celebrate ten years of devolution. All these children were born in Scotland on 1 July 1999 – the same day as the Parliament. In 2009 they travelled to Holyrood from as far away as the Faroe Islands, Germany and the USA to hear the Queen speak to Parliament and to be presented to her.

Their other treats were inventing a new computer game, making cupcakes, and designing their own tartan ceramic tile.

Scottish Youth Parliament

'Young people are part of the solution, not the problem.'

Scottish Youth Parliament

The Scottish Youth Parliament (SYP) encourages young people to engage with important matters. It's a channel for alerting politicians about what Scotland's youth is passionate about. The Members of SYP even produce a youth manifesto every four years prior to the elections. One of their objectives is to lower the voting age from the current 18 years of age to 16 years.

SYP is a young people's parliament – members are aged between 14 and 25. They are democratically elected, and independent of political parties. The Youth Parliament is inclusive, believing that all young people can share their opinions, whatever their background. For more on the **Scottish Youth Parliament**, visit **www.syp.org.uk.**

Your voice, your future!

Public speakers often used to challenge the passing pedestrians at the foot of the Mound, in Edinburgh – standing on a soap-box. One of the challenges in the *Festival of Politics 2010* was for young people to 'get up on their soapbox'. The event, chaired by Scotland's Commissioner for Children and Young People, proposed a 'two-minute manifesto' on 'What would most change their lives for the better?' Why not try this?

The Scottish Parliament sometimes hosts the Youth Parliament's meetings in the Debating Chamber. Other events for young people held here include an annual St Andrew's Day debate and a testing Euroquiz.

Grant Costello (SYP Chair), Robin Parker (President, NUS Scotland) and members of the Scottish Youth Parliament celebrating the announcement that 16-year-olds would be given the vote in the Scottish Independence Referendum.

Open the Doors!

Open the doors! Light of the day, shine in;
  light of the mind, shine out!

We have a building which is more than a building.
  There is a commerce between inner and outer,
    between brightness and shadow,
      between the world and those who think about the world.

Is it not a mystery? The parts cohere, they come together
  like petals of a flower,
    yet they also send their tongues outward
      to feel and taste the teeming earth.
Did you want classic columns and predictable pediments?
  A growl of old Gothic grandeur? A blissfully boring box?
Not here, no thanks! No icon, no IKEA, no iceberg,
  but curves and caverns, nooks and niches,
    huddles and heavens, syncopations and surprises.
      Leave symmetry to the cemetery.
But bring together slate and stainless steel,
  black granite and grey granite,
    seasoned oak and sycamore,
      concrete blond and smooth as silk –
    the mix is almost alive – it breathes and beckons –
      imperial marble it is not!

Edwin Morgan

Read more

To the left are the opening lines of Edwin Morgan's hymn to democracy, read at the official opening of the new Parliament building. You can read the entire poem in *100 Favourite Scottish Poems to Read Out Loud* (Luath Press, 2007).

Comfortably Scottish

Perhaps a closing word could come from a well-kent BBC political journalist who often reports from Holyrood:

'There are Gaelic Scots and Irish Scots and Asian Scots. Like most nations, we are a splendidly chaotic mix. Being Scottish is not a question of language or ethnic origin or any other single factor. It is a question of choice. We have become comfortably Scottish.'

Brian Taylor, 2002

ANSWERS

Page 8: **Mony a mickle maks a muckle** – Lots of little bits add up to something big (*or*, if you look after the pennies, the pounds will take care of themselves).

Page 9: **The Darien Scheme** – In 1697, Darien, near Panama, Central America, was one of Scotland's first attempts at overseas colonisation. The site was unwise. It was a very unhealthy part of the world in those days, it was already a Spanish territory, and in order not to antagonise Spain, the British King William instructed nearby Dutch and English colonies not to supply the settlement. Darien quickly failed, with serious loss of life and catastrophic loss of money. Scotland was left almost bankrupt, a situation which made the prospect of Union with England all the more prudent. The chest, *c.*1695, with its complex locking system is a strong box that held money and documents of the Company of Scotland which funded the Darien Scheme.

Page 14: **Quick question** – The question of future devolution for Scotland, Wales and Northern Ireland is interesting. Each of the three 'minority' components of the Union could respond to the future of devolution in a different way. Some may push for more devolution, some may choose independence, and some may wish to retain the existing status quo.

Page 17: **Think about it** – Scotland's renewables include ample water-power, with not only freshwater resources for hydro-electric dams and watermills on rivers, but also tidal and wave resources around its lengthy coast-line. It also has wind power and solar power. A mix of these would probably be the wisest guarantee of safe and renewable energy supplies.

Page 23: **Think about it** – Democracy is government by the people, for the people. (Greek *demos* = the people; *kratos* = strength.) The people hold the power by electing representatives such as councillors, MSPs and MPs. A democracy aims to have equality of rights.

Page 29: **Debating techniques** – The speaker who shouts the loudest is not necessarily presenting the best argument! Debating techniques include: knowing what you want to say and being confident in saying it; knowing your audience; ensuring your talk has a beginning, middle and an end; and above all, listening to other people's opinions.

Page 31: **Pulling in the votes** – Look at the online SYP Monthly Updates at **www.syp.org.uk** to keep up-to-date with some recent issues.

Page 33: **Making cuts – less is more** – Study recent news headlines related to how money is spent by government. Is there an area where you think money can be saved?

Page 37: **Mystery object** – A medal commemorating the opening of the Scottish Parliament presented to all babies born in Scotland on 1 July 1999.

ANSWERS – Facts and activities section

Page iii: **On the trail of Robert the Bruce** – see map.

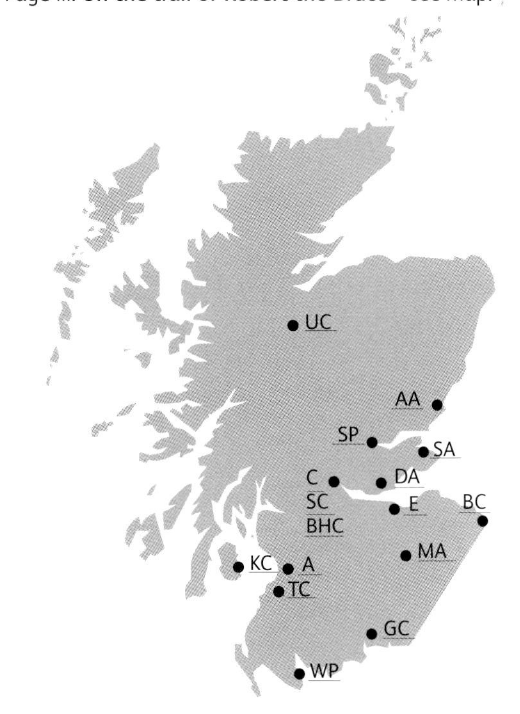

Page v: **Wordsearch** – Answers below.

T	T	L	Q	D	P	E	L	I	M	L	A	Y	O	R
E	H	S	U	R	E	A	S	R	E	B	M	A	H	C
E	N	R	E	T	V	V	R	G	N	I	T	O	V	L
T	C	A	E	Y	B	B	O	L	N	E	D	R	A	G
T	E	R	N	E	S	D	G	L	I	N	E	L	S	S
I	T	N	S	G	H	A	O	B	U	A	L	L	I	B
M	M	I	B	P	N	O	M	O	R	T	M	L	O	N
M	G	G	E	E	T	I	N	A	R	G	I	E	N	O
O	H	M	R	G	O	C	T	O	C	Y	E	O	N	I
C	L	H	R	O	C	W	D	A	U	E	L	T	N	T
L	O	C	Y	L	A	L	D	T	B	R	M	O	L	I
R	E	I	D	S	C	L	O	S	E	E	S	C	H	L
E	T	A	G	N	O	N	A	C	F	I	D	B	M	A
H	O	R	S	D	N	Y	W	E	S	R	O	H	A	O
A	B	B	A	L	L	O	T	P	A	P	E	R	N	C

The odd one out is the Granite Egg because it is not mentioned in the text. This polished granite sculpture of a large pink-footed goose egg was a gift from the Parliament of Iceland, symbolising the friendship between the two parliaments. The pink-footed goose spends its summers in Iceland and migrates every winter to Scotland.

There shall be a Scottish Parliament

Facts and activities

The opening of the first Parliament of King James VII, Edinburgh, 1685.

Write a haiku

Write a haiku on the Scottish Parliament.
It's only a three-line poem, but there is a certain sound pattern to it.

1st line – should have 5 sounds (or syllables)
2nd line – should have 7 sounds
3rd line – should have 5 sounds

The finished haiku is like a miniature painting or snapshot of a scene. You could refer, as a starting point, to some of the variety of materials used in the Scottish Parliament building.

- Sparkling Aberdeenshire granite used on the façades
- Sturdy Caithness stone used for the flooring
- Scottish oak at the centre of the Debating Chamber
- Red pantiles and grey slate on the roof of Queensberry House
- Polished concrete in the Main Hall
- Stainless steel used on some of the roofs
- Italian marble floors in the Black and White Corridor

Don't worry if all your words don't fit the 5 – 7 – 5 sound pattern at first. It soon comes with practice! Here's one to start you thinking:

Three fluttering flags
Greet you on your arrival
At this unique place.

A Scottish Parliament haiku

....

....

....

On the trail of Robert the Bruce

These places are all connected with King Robert, the Bruce. He held a Parliament or Assembly in many of them with his nobles and clergy.

Mark the initial letters on the map in the correct place.

Answers on page 40.

AA: Arbroath Abbey (Declaration of Arbroath 1320)

A: Ayr (Assembly here)

BHC: Bannockburn Heritage Centre (outside Stirling)

BC: Berwick-upon-Tweed (3 Parliaments)

C: Cambuskenneth Priory (by Stirling)

DA: Dunfermline Abbey (burial place of Bruce)

E: Edinburgh Castle and Holyrood (3 Parliaments)

GC: Greyfriars Chapel, Dumfries (where Bruce killed John Comyn)

KC: King's Cave, Arran (where Bruce watched the spider struggle to spin its web)

MA: Melrose Abbey (final burial place of Bruce's embalmed heart)

SA: St Andrews (1 Parliament)

SC: Stirling Castle (1 Parliament here and 2 at Cambuskenneth)

SP: Scone Palace, Perthshire (where Bruce was crowned in 1306; 4 Parliaments here and one in Perth)

TC: Turnberry Castle (where Bruce was born in 1274)

UC: Urquhart Castle (important during Bruce's struggle for independence)

WP: Whithorn Priory (Bruce went there on a pilgrimage in 1329, a few months before he died)

Windpower: Yes or No?

Read the facts carefully. Choose which side you take – *Yes* or *No*.

Points against wind farms	Points in favour of wind farms
✻ Wind farms are noisy	✻ Windpower is one of the cleanest forms of energy
✻ New giant turbines would be 140 metres high – that's taller than Big Ben	✻ Scotland is one of the windiest countries in Europe
✻ They make it difficult for walkers to roam in the countryside	✻ Present windpower reduces the annual amount of carbon dioxide by 1 million tonnes (the equivalent of taking 300,000 cars off the road)
✻ The best places for wind farms are furthest from large centres of population	✻ 1 modern wind turbine can supply 1000 homes with electricity
✻ Giant turbines harm flight paths of migrating birds	✻ Wind farms will only be built on 0.5 % of Scotland's land area

- Design a campaign advertisement for a Scottish newspaper.
- The aim is to persuade people one way or another.
- Think of a catchy slogan.
- Use some of the facts above in your advertisement.
- Draw a picture or cartoon to illustrate the message you are putting across.

Wordsearch

These are places, things or phrases related to or near the Scottish Parliament. Can you find them in the wordsearch? Which one is the odd one out? [Clue: It can be found in the Scottish Parliament Garden, and was a gift from the Icelandic Parliament.]

Answers on page 40

ACT
BALLOT PAPER
BILL
CANONGATE
CHAMBERS
COALITION
COMMITTEE
DEBATING
DEVOLUTION
GARDEN LOBBY
GRANITE EGG
HORSE WYND
MACE
PARLIAMENT
QUEENSBERRY
REIDS CLOSE
ROYAL MILE
THREE HONOURS
VOTING

T	T	L	Q	D	P	E	L	I	M	L	A	Y	O	R
E	H	S	U	R	E	A	S	R	E	B	M	A	H	C
E	N	R	E	T	V	V	R	G	N	I	T	O	V	L
T	C	A	E	Y	B	B	O	L	N	E	D	R	A	G
T	E	R	N	E	S	D	G	L	I	N	E	L	S	S
I	T	N	S	G	H	A	O	B	U	A	L	L	I	B
M	M	I	B	P	N	O	M	O	R	T	M	L	O	N
M	G	G	E	E	T	I	N	A	R	G	I	E	N	O
O	H	M	R	G	O	C	T	O	C	Y	E	O	N	I
C	L	H	R	O	C	W	D	A	U	E	L	T	N	T
L	O	C	Y	L	A	L	D	T	B	R	M	O	L	I
R	E	I	D	S	C	L	O	S	E	E	S	C	H	L
E	T	A	G	N	O	N	A	C	F	I	D	B	M	A
H	O	R	S	D	N	Y	W	E	S	R	O	H	A	O
A	B	B	A	L	L	O	T	P	A	P	E	R	N	C

You can move diagonally, as well as up and down, or straight across, in any direction, to find the listed words.

Name challenge

Find out the names and political parties of these people who govern *you*.

Name of First Minister and Party

Name of Deputy First Minister and Party

Name of Scottish Parliament List Constituency, List MSPs and Parties

Name of Scottish Parliament Constituency, MSP and Party

Name of Prime Minister and Party

Name of Leader of the Opposition and Party

Name of Member of Parliament (Westminster), Constituency and Party

Name of Member of European Parliament (MEP) and Party

Community Council name and Chairperson

Regional Council name, Councillor(s) and Chairperson

The Union Flag

There are two theories about the origin of the name 'Union Jack'.

Some say the name derives from the fact that the flag was flown from the jackstaff, a small mast in the bows of British warships. Others thought it was named after James VI and I of Great Britain (*Jacobus* is Latin for James). He introduced the flag after he inherited the English throne in 1603.

Various designs were drawn up for a common flag. Which flag should be hoisted above the king's ships? In 1606 the national flags of Scotland and England were united for use at sea – this made the first 'Union Jack'.

When the red St George's cross of England was put onto the white cross of St Andrew (saltire), a white border was added around the red cross. This was because the rules of heraldry demanded that two colours must never touch each other.

In 1707, in the reign of Queen Anne, the Union Flag was made the national flag for use ashore and afloat by Royal Proclamation. Scotland and England now not only shared a monarch, but also a parliament.

The St Patrick's cross was not added until 1801 when the three national flags combined to make up the Union Jack as we know it today.

But amazingly enough, no law has ever been passed making it the national flag. It's still officially a flag of the monarch, rather than the Union.

Here is the Union Jack as we know it today.

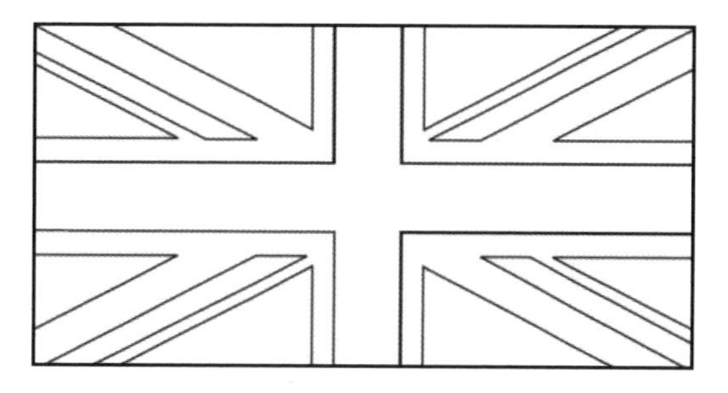

Can you colour it in correctly?

USEFUL WEBSITE

The Scottish Parliament: **www.scottish.parliament.uk**

From the home page you can go on an online tour of the Scottish Parliament and explore a MSP's office, the Debating Chamber and Committee Rooms by clicking on:

Visit & Learn
Explore Parliament
Virtual Tours

You require Java to be enabled on your system to view the virtual tours.

Or watch the Parliament debates and its committees live on the web by clicking on:

News & Media Centre
Parliament TV

If you want to attend a meeting of the Parliament, either phone Visitor Services at 0131–348 5200 (freephone 0800 092 7600) or email:

sp.bookings@scottishparliament.uk

PLACES OF INTEREST

These places are either mentioned in this book or have strong connections to our present Scottish Parliament. Always check the opening times online or with the local Tourist Office.

Angus
Arbroath Abbey (Historic Scotland). Exhibition on the Declaration of Arbroath.

Borders
Melrose Abbey (Historic Scotland).

Edinburgh
Scottish Parliament at Holyrood.
Edinburgh Castle (Historic Scotland).
Parliament Hall, Signet Library.
National Museum of Scotland, Chambers Street.

Fife
Dunfermline Abbey and Palace (Historic Scotland).
Falkland Palace (National Trust).
St Andrews University (Parliament Hall).

Highland
Urquhart Castle, Loch Ness (Historic Scotland).

Perthshire
Scone Palace, near Perth.

South West Scotland
Robert the Bruce Trail, Dumfries and Galloway.
Savings Banks Museum, Ruthwell (on the Solway Coast Heritage Trail).
Glenluce Abbey, Galloway (Historic Scotland).
Whithorn Priory and Museum (Historic Scotland).

Stirling
Stirling Castle (Historic Scotland).
Bannockburn Heritage Centre (National Trust).
Cambuskenneth Abbey (Historic Scotland).

West of Scotland
People's Palace, Glasgow (social history museum).
Whitelee Wind Farm Visitor Centre (the largest land-based wind farm in Europe).

FURTHER CREDITS

ILLUSTRATION CREDITS

© ANGUS COUNCIL – for page 4 (Declaration of Arbroath re-enactment).
BIBLIOTHEQUE NATIONALE – for page 6 (Mary and Francis, RGA-08757 NAL82, folio 154v).
CASSELLS OLD AND NEW EDINBURGH: Its History, its People and its Places by James Grant (Cassell & Co.: London, n.d.) – for pages 7 (Parliament Square); 11 (John Stuart, Robert Burns, Adam Smith); 28 (Old Parliament Hall).
© HOLLY CRUISE – for page 2 (Three Estates cartoons).
HISTORIC SCOTLAND – © Crown Copyright Historic Scotland, reproduced courtesy of Historic Scotland. www.historicscotlandimages.gov.uk – for pages 3 (Parliament Hall, Stirling Castle); 25 (original Honours of Scotland).
© GORDON JARVIE – for page 22 (upturned boat).
NATIONAL GALLERIES OF SCOTLAND – for pages 5 (© William Hole, Battle of Bannockburn frieze, Scottish National Portrait Gallery); 10 (© James Drummond, *The Porteous Mob*, National Gallery of Scotland); 20 (Sir Henry Raeburn, *Reverend Robert Walker* [1755–1808] *skating on Duddingston Loch*, National Gallery of Scotland); 27 (Unknown artist, James IV, Scottish National Portrait Gallery).
NATIONAL MUSEUMS SCOTLAND (© National Museums Scotland) for pages 5 (seal); 8 (brooch, fan); 9 (safe, engraving); 10 (axe); 11 (shop sign); 12 (brooch); 13 (Suffragettes); 14 (mug, poster); 16 (ration books/coupons, oil rig); 17 (vigil, leaflets); 18 (Parliament opening; procession); 19 (mace, Donald Dewar, Winnie Ewing); 21 (Wet Review); 23 (Riding of Parliament); 31 (leaflet); 37 (medal) – Facts and activities section page i (Downsitting of Parliament).
LYNNE REILLY – for pages 7 (flags); 21 (wall); 23 (proverb); 25 (quote); 26 (Canongate Wall); 30 (polling place); 33 (Victoria Quay); 35 (John Knox House, windows); 39 (Parliament building) – Facts and activities section pages iv (wind turbines); v (Queensberry House).
© RENEWABLE DEVICES SWIFT TURBINES LTD – for page 17 (turbine).
THE SCOTTISH PARLIAMENT – for pages 21 (windows); 22 (Queensberry House and Garden Lobby); 23 (Parliament building); 24 (Parliament opening); 25 (Three Honours sculpture); 26 (logo); 27 (Public Gallery); 28 (Nicola Sturgeon); 29 (New Debating Chamber); 32 (Parliament exterior); 34 (Committee Room); 35 (MSP's office); 37 (Parliament roof); 39 (Queensberry House). All images © Scottish Parliamentary Corporate Body 2013.
SCOTTISH YOUTH PARLIAMENT for page 38 (campaign). Image © Scottish Youth Parliament 2013.
SCRAN © NEWSQUEST [*Herald & Times*]. Licensor www.scran.ac.uk – for page 16 (Winnie Ewing, 1967 Campaign).
SCRAN © Colin McPherson. Licensor www.scran.ac.uk – for page 20 (Enric Miralles, Donald Dewar).

TEXT CREDITS

BEING SCOTTISH: PERSONAL REFLECTIONS ON SCOTTISH IDENTITY TODAY by Tom Devine and Paddy Logue (eds) (Edinburgh: Polygon, 2002) – for page 39 (Brian Taylor quote).
VOYAGE OF INTENT: SONNETS AND ESSAYS FROM THE SCOTTISH PARLIAMENT by James Robertson (Edinburgh: Luath Press, 2005) and *100 FAVOURITE SCOTTISH POEMS TO READ OUT LOUD* by Gordon Jarvie (ed.) (Luath Press, 2007) – for page 39 (excerpt from Edwin Morgan's poem 'Open the Doors!').

OTHER TITLES IN THE SCOTTIES SERIES

(Frances and Gordon Jarvie, editors)

The Clans (Gordon Jarvie)
The Covenanters (Claire Watts)
Flight in Scotland (Frances and Gordon Jarvie)
Greyfriars Bobby: A Tale of Victorian Edinburgh (Frances and Gordon Jarvie)
The Jacobites (Antony Kamm)
Mary, Queen of Scots (Elizabeth Douglas)
Robert Burns in Time and Place (Frances and Gordon Jarvie)
The Romans in Scotland (Frances Jarvie)
Scotland's Vikings (Frances and Gordon Jarvie)
Scottish Explorers (Antony Kamm)
Scottish Rocks and Fossils (Alan and Moira McKirdy)
Scottish Kings and Queens (Elizabeth Douglas)
Supernatural Scotland (Eileen Dunlop)